by **Neil McGowan**

www.stagerights.com

DISPOSABLE NECESSITIES

For all stage performance inquiries, please contact:

Steele Spring Stage Rights
3845 Cazador Street
Los Angeles, CA 90065
(323) 739-0413
www.stagerights.com

DISPOSABLE NECESSITIES

ORIGINAL PRODUCTION CREDITS

Disposable Necessities was produced at Rogue Machine Theatre in Venice, CA in December 2019.

Produced by John Perrin Flynn

Directed by Guillermo Cienfuegos

Cast List:

Daniel Totten.................................... Darrett Sanders
Al Totten .... Billy Flynn
Phillip Fain.................................... Claire Blackwelder
Chadwick Totten .... Jefferson Reid
Dee Totten... Ann Noble

DISPOSABLE NECESSITIES

CHARACTER DESCRIPTIONS

Casting Requirements: 2F, 3M

DANIEL TOTTEN – 55, male, Caucasian: Appears to be 55 years old but, in actuality, is 80 and feels twice that old. Once a hugely successful novelist, he is now being kept alive financially by his wife. His current body was once a solid, magnificent thing, but now is as weathered and beaten down as his state of mind.

AL TOTTEN – 35, Male, any ethnicity: Daniel's wife, Alice, appears to be a handsome 35-year-old man. In reality, she is 90 years old and experiencing the prime of her life. Power and wealth suits her, but perhaps a little too well.

CHADWICK TOTTEN – 24, male, African American: Daniel and Al's son is the eternal adolescent, despite just turning 53. His birthday gift from mom is a nice, shiny, young body to spend the next five or six years in, because Chad would rather die than ever be over 30.

DEE TOTTEN – 50, female, Caucasian: Deandra is Daniel and Alice's estranged daughter. She is 50 years old in appearance and reality, because she has refused all her life to engage in the body-swapping activities the rest of her family has profited from. She is a writer like her dad, but never nearly as successful.

PHILLIP FAIN – 22, female, any ethnicity: Phillip was once a short, overweight, slovenly man that lost most of his hair in his late teens. With the benefit of a very large trust fund, in his 55 years he has been able to experience many times over the luxury of being ridiculously attractive. His current physique is that of a gorgeous young woman, exactly the kind he used to prey on.

SETTING

A large metropolitan area in the United States, in the year 2095.

RUNNING TIME

2 hours

ACT 1

SCENE 1

In the darkness, set to a 1990s indie rock song, we see a projection of a photograph of a man in his early 30s and his wife, with a five-year-old boy and a three-year-old girl. After a moment, that photograph swipes to the left to reveal another photo of the same family a couple years later. Then another, the happy family on vacation.

Lights up on the living room of a luxury high rise apartment with ultramodern furniture and large windows that look out to a view of a futuristic cityscape. DANIEL TOTTEN (55 years old) is splayed out on the sofa, drinking a bottle of club soda, staring out into space. He is clearly not the man in the photos, still visible to us above his head. He swipes the air in front of him which brings up a new photo, this one of the man and his young daughter in his arms. Daniel's arm drops and he stares at this photo. Then:

The music fades and the photo disappears as AL TOTTEN enters through the front door, a handsome man, mid-30s, sharp business suit. A bit harried at the moment, but relieved to some extent by the sight of Daniel on the couch, who hasn't noticed the presence of another.

AL: Daniel. Honey.

Daniel is oblivious, still looking at the photo, his foot still tapping to the music that we no longer hear.

(Louder)

Daniel!

AL comes around to his line of sight, arms waving, getting his attention. Daniel taps his temple. We hear a COMPUTER TONE.

DANIEL: I had music on.

AL: I gathered. Listen—

DANIEL: I must have lost track of time. Is it already—

AL: I'm home early. I tried calling you.

DANIEL: You know I go offline when I'm writing, Al.

AL picks up a notepad from off the couch and displays the clean front page.

AL: That's working out well for you.

DANIEL: You don't understand the creative process.

DANIEL snatches the notebook away as AL goes to the wet bar to pour a tall glass of wine.

AL: Aren't you waiting for that call from your agent?

DANIEL: He can leave a message. I didn't get to where I am so I can sit around waiting to hear from a parasite in a tie.

AL: You need to check in occasionally.

DANIEL: I don't have to do anything. He works for me!

AL: I meant in general. It's not a good idea to be so isolated all the time.

DANIEL: This from you? Where do you ever go or speak to anyone that isn't shop talk?

AL: I talk to you every day.

DANIEL: Mostly about work.

AL: I'm just saying you need to be reachable. What if there's an emergency?

DANIEL becomes alarmed.

DANIEL: Why are you home?

AL: I tried to call you.

DANIEL: Al?

AL: Calm down. I wanted to tell you before you heard it somewhere else.

DANIEL: Heard what, Al?

AL: Take a breath.

DANIEL: I'm going online.

He opens a virtual window in front of his face and starts poking and swiping the air. AL comes to him and physically restrains him.

AL: Stop, Daniel. I'll tell you. Just don't overreact.

DANIEL: What happened?

AL: It's Chadwick. He had... something of an accident.

DANIEL: Was it serious?

AL: Well, he's dead.

DANIEL goes pale. He walks past AL to the wet bar.

Breathe, Daniel. Just calm down, baby.

DANIEL: I'm having a perfectly reasonable reaction to the death of our son. Can I just have that, please?

He opens a bottle of club soda and downs it.

AL: Fine, have your moment. But it's obviously not as bad as all that. He's being downloaded right this moment.

DANIEL: He is?

AL: We'll have him back by tomorrow.

DANIEL: You were able to get him a new module that quickly?

AL: We picked it out weeks ago. Oops...

Getting it, he gives AL a hard look.

It was his birthday yesterday, remember? Did you remember that?

DANIEL's reaction suggests that he did not.

DANIEL: This accident just coincidentally happened on his birthday?

AL: He wanted a new module for his birthday, so—

DANIEL: How did it happen?

AL: Why does that matter?

DANIEL: The timing seems awfully suspicious.

AL: He fell out of a helicopter.

DANIEL takes this in.

DANIEL: He...

AL: Fell. Out of a helicopter.

DANIEL *(shakes his head, not even sure what to ask next)*: I....where?

AL: 5,000 feet into the Chesapeake Bay.

DANIEL: Accidentally, huh?

AL: As far as the authorities are concerned. Right, Daniel?

(A beat)

It's called Thrilling Out. When you know you have a new module lined up, you go out in a blaze of glory. All the kids are doing it.

DANIEL: Chadwick is 53 years old.

AL: Fifty-four, Daniel. I agree it's ridiculous and wasteful. And I certainly wouldn't expect you to understand.

DANIEL: What is that supposed to mean?

AL: Obviously you believe in holding on to these things an absurdly long time. That's your preference. Chadwick doesn't like being over thirty. He's terrified he'll have a heart attack or something.

DANIEL: He just got the body he was in!

AL: That was five years ago. In any case, the next time you see your son, he'll be a bright, shiny 24-year-old.

DANIEL: It didn't occur to you to consult me on this?

AL: I didn't want to bother you with something so silly. And don't worry about the cost. I have a handle on our finances, dear. Momma's got it covered.

She gives him a peck on the cheek, more patronizing than intended.

AL (CONT'D): I need to get back to the office. You can go back to your... writing.

AL exits to the hallway, yelling out to him.

How are your eyes?

DANIEL: My eyes?

AL (O.S.): Are you still having trouble reading? You need to see a doctor.

DANIEL has picked up the wine cork left behind by AL, staring at it.

DANIEL: There's nothing a doctor can do. This is what happens to bodies at this age. The eyes go. And ears. And everything else.

DANIEL brings the cork to his nose and he inhales it deeply.

AL (O.S.): It's ridiculous. They tell you these things will last for 80 years or more, but they neglect to say that everything will go to shit halfway through.

A DOORBELL.

Can you get that, Daniel?

He goes to the door and opens it, revealing a young, very pretty woman. She says nothing, just stares at him.

DANIEL: Can I help you?

GIRL: Are you really going to pretend you don't know me?

DANIEL: I'm sorry, I–

GIRL: You bastard.

DANIEL: Excuse me? How did you get past building security? You can't just knock on peoples' doors–

GIRL: Fuck you, Danny!

She pushes past him and into the suite.

DANIEL: I'm sorry, I really don't... I'm trying to place you.

AL enters.

AL: Who was it?

Seeing the girl:

Who is this?

DANIEL: I don't know.

AL: We don't want any cookies, honey.

GIRL: You must be Alice.

AL: Must I.

GIRL: I feel like I already know you. Danny and I never meant to hurt you.

DANIEL: We what?

AL: Who is this child, Daniel?

DANIEL: I promise you Alice, I don't—

GIRL: I wanted us all to be in the same room. It's time we get everything out and in the open. It's time for honesty. Right, Danny?

AL: Um, Danny? Can you tell me what the fuck is going on here?

GIRL: It's time she knows everything.

She puts both hands on her belly, looks down at it and back up at him.

Everything.

DANIEL: Whoa. Uh—

GIRL: I want us to be a family. The three of us. In nine months, the four of us.

AL: This isn't happening.

GIRL: We can all have dinner together every night, and sleep together in a big bed. Wouldn't that be so beautiful?

DANIEL sees a look in AL's eyes that causes alarm.

DANIEL: Hold on a second...

AL grabs an ice pick from the wet bar.

GIRL: Whoa.

AL: You're going to watch me stab her to death, and then you're next.

GIRL: Okay, time out!

AL begins chasing her.

DANIEL: Alice, wait!

AL: Fuck you! You betrayed 55 years of marriage on this walking ball of pocket lint with a vagina?

GIRL: Hey, guys, let's take a second. Dan, I—

AL starts toward her with the poker. DANIEL jumps between them, holding a chair.

DANIEL: Hold on hold on hold on.

AL: I'm going to kill you painfully, download you into a new module, and kill you again!

DANIEL: Alice, calm down! I have a feeling I know what's going on here.

AL watches as DANIEL takes the girl aside, looks her in the eyes, and then holds out his hand. The girl lets out a laugh, and shakes his hand. There is an audible COMPUTER TONE.

You asshole.

AL: Who is this?

DANIEL: Alice, meet our old friend Phil Fain, playing a little joke on us.

AL *(drops the ice pick, laughs with maniacal joy)*: Phillip, you unbelievable bastard!

PHILLIP: That got real! That got real real!

PHILLIP and AL embrace.

AL: I genuinely almost murdered you!

PHILLIP: You weren't playing around! You were going to kill me, your husband, and our unborn child!

They continue laughing. DANIEL does not.

I was just coming to mess with Dan, and then you walked in, and I figured, screw it, I'll just roll with it. I can't believe I caught you both at home.

DANIEL *(dryly)*: What luck.

AL: Phillip! Look at you!

PHILLIP shows off his body, curtseying, doing a spin.

DANIEL: Christ.

PHILLIP: I did it. I really went for it.

AL: You look fantastic, Phillip. I love it.

PHILLIP: Thank you, my dear.

AL: Come on, Daniel. You can't deny he looks amazing.

DANIEL: I'm not about to tell my friend of over 60 years that he has a nice tight ass.

AL: Don't be offended. His eyes barely work.

DANIEL: I can see fine.

PHILLIP: It's fine, I get it. At his age it's difficult to appreciate someone on any kind of sexual level. I might as well be an orangutan in a burka.

He playfully punches Daniel in the arm.

AL: How in the world did you score this?

PHILLIP: Right place, right time. I went to the showroom on a whim a week ago. Absolutely no intention of getting a new one. And of course the inventory was all picked over. They were all too old or used up or had a weird mole or something.

AL: Good ones are getting harder and harder to find.

PHILLIP: So you gotta jump when you get lucky. They brought her in straight from the morgue as I was just about to leave. Not a mark on her. Drank herself to death. Frat party!

AL: Jackpot!

PHILLIP: Decent price, too. Her parents or whatever must have been pretty desperate to collect. So, I went all in. I'd never seriously considered going for a female module, but—

AL: How could you resist?

PHILLIP: Come on. Look at this shit.

He flaunts it again. DANIEL looks ill.

I made the down payment right there, signed everything. They prepped the body, loaded the hardware into her brain, got a hold of the people at Life Forever Industries and cut through the red tape, and the download from the Heaven Database started within a couple hours. I didn't even bother looking at the old module again before I high-tailed it out of there on these sexy little legs.

AL: You had some good times in that thing.

PHILLIP: Yeah, but in the end, it's just a lump of meat and bones, right? You know, when I got downloaded the first time, it was so strange, looking down at the body I was born in, lying there on that metal table. Remember that thing? Man, I was a toad!

AL *(laughs hysterically)*: You really were! Like Danny DeVito, in a funhouse mirror.

PHILLIP: I hated being ugly. I would've paid anything to be good looking.

DANIEL: And you did. Three times over.

PHILLIP: And worth every penny. Time for you to catch up, old timer.

AL: He is due, isn't he? I keep telling him.

PHILLIP: Do yourself a favor, brother. God damn, you forget how great it is to be young. I bent down to pick up a sock this morning, bracing myself for a world of pain, and you know what it felt like? Luxurious. It felt sumptuous to bend over. When I wake up in the morning, I feel like a billion bucks, instead of feeling like I fought in a battle while I slept. And good god, do I smell amazing. My goddamn body, and my hair. How do women concentrate, walking around smelling so good all the time?

AL: I do miss that. The way my female bodies smelled.

DANIEL: I miss it too.

An awkward silence. Finally:

Congratulations, Phil. I hope only the best for you in this living, breathing impulse purchase.

PHILLIP: That's the spirit! Let's celebrate.

AL: I wish I could, but I have to get back to the office. Phillip, congratulations. If you need any help with—

PHILLIP: The female stuff? I'll do that. They gave me a nice little pamphlet, but—

AL: If it's as vague as the one they give you for a male module, you're going to need plenty of guidance.

She has gathered her things and heads for the door.

Have fun, boys. Or... you know.

AL blows DANIEL a kiss and exits in a rush. Daniel and PHILLIP take each other in.

PHILLIP: It's been a while, hombre!

DANIEL: I've been busy. It's good to see you, Phil.

PHILLIP: Likewise. I'd say you look great, but... meh.

DANIEL gives him a polite smile and heads to the wet bar.

DANIEL: Drink?

PHILLIP: I'd love one.

DANIEL: Unfortunately, so would I.

PHILLIP: Hey, do you...

DANIEL: Huh?

PHILLIP: I'm finding I don't like whiskey as much as I did. Do you maybe have white wine?

DANIEL rolls his eyes, pours PHILLIP some wine and opens himself a bottle of club soda. Phillip has made himself comfortable on the sofa and begins rubbing his smooth legs with his hands.

DANIEL: Phil. Come on, man.

PHILLIP: Sorry! I can't keep my hands off. I swear to god, I went straight home and spent the whole first day just playing with myself.

DANIEL: Christ.

PHILLIP: Look at these tits. I barely need a bra. They're so perky. You wanna touch them?

DANIEL: We need to immediately set some very clear boundaries.

PHILLIP: You're never gonna catch up to this brave new world, are you? I don't get it, Danny. You did this once, and you seemed to like it. Alice has done it three times, your son has done it, how many times now?

DANIEL: I've lost count.

PHILLIP: You've got one new body under your belt, but your brain will always be old-fashioned.

DANIEL: My talent for romanticizing an earlier time has served me well, thank you very much.

PHILLIP: It worked for you for a while. Back when nostalgia was popular.

DANIEL *(nostalgically)*: The good old days.

PHILLIP: Look, I know this is nuts. I hate not being able to pee standing up and obviously it's only a matter of time before I become a horrible driver. But I don't regret it for a second. It's so liberating, Danny. I can get away with saying and doing literally almost anything. I slapped a random guy in the face on the street today for no reason, and demanded he apologize to me. And he did!

DANIEL: God have mercy on us all.

PHILLIP: So I'm a chick now. Big deal. In case you haven't noticed, your wife has a dick.

DANIEL: I noticed.

PHILLIP: You learned to accept that. You'll learn to love this.

DANIEL: I never said I accepted it.

PHILLIP: Seriously? Here all this time I thought you were this supremely open-minded guy.

DANIEL: Surprise.

PHILLIP: Why'd you let it happen?

DANIEL: I didn't have a choice.

PHILLIP: You bought her the body, right?

DANIEL: Spent almost every dime we had. Right around the time my career was stalling.

PHILLIP: So why'd you do it?

DANIEL *(a beat; then he starts)*: We were still in the house out in Elkridge. Remember?

PHILLIP: I only made it out there a few times. Old houses in the middle of the woods make me uneasy.

DANIEL: It was a strong, sturdy manor built with care, out of real, solid materials, on five acres of grass and trees. A dream house I was able to realize through my accomplishments.

PHILLIP: I remember it smelled kind of musty.

DANIEL: Anyway, I was sitting in my den one evening, and I heard a terrible noise. I thought I was home alone. Alice had been working so much around that time. She had just started at the agency a year earlier. The real estate market was booming, and her company was doing great, but she wasn't making any headway, you know? Anyway, she would often come home after a full day just to change and then go back out for more without bothering me. I didn't know what I'd just heard, but I ran out into the foyer and... found her, crumpled on the floor. In so much pain.

PHILLIP: What happened?

DANIEL: That module she was in, her second one... it was tall and gorgeous, but so clumsy. Especially in high heels. The grand staircase in that house was made of real hard oak.

DANIEL (CONT'D): She was in a hurry and she just... tripped, or slipped, at the top, and went right down. Hit every step on the way. Broken bones, head trauma, internal bleeding.

PHILLIP: I can't believe I don't remember this!

DANIEL: We never told anyone. Next thing I knew, we were in the ambulance. They were about to put her into an induced coma, with little hope of her ultimately surviving, and with what little energy she could muster, she begged me to download her into a male module. I was floored. She'd never said anything like that before. I thought she was delirious. She swore it would help her in the business world. I told her, honey, this is practically the 22nd century, things like that don't matter. But she made me promise. And so I did.

PHILLIP: You're a good man, Danny.

DANIEL: Uh, yeah, right back at ya, pal. Anyway, turns out maybe she was right. Within a year, she was running that place.

He looks around.

Good thing, too. We almost lost it all. This is all hers.

PHILLIP: Seriously?

DANIEL: I still get the occasional paltry royalty check. I treat myself to a popsicle.

PHILLIP: Got anything new coming out?

DANIEL: No publishers seem to care about any of my new books, which is awfully polite of them, considering I haven't been in much of a mood to write any.

PHILLIP: You had a good run. I sure didn't hack it as a writer for very long. Luckily I have a natural talent for living on a ridiculously large trust fund.

DANIEL: We all have our gifts.

PHILLIP: Cheers to that, brother.

DANIEL: I am waiting on some big news, actually. There's a possibility of a large re-release of my entire canon. I'm trying not to get my hopes up about it, but... I'm failing.

PHILLIP: I hope the best for you, but why would anyone believe that a bunch of books written fifty years ago that take place twenty years before we were even born could be popular again? No offense, but I found it hard to believe they were such big hits the first time around.

DANIEL: Becoming a hot piece of ass has made you a real dickhead, Phil. The 1990s were an interesting time. The end of the middle class. The final days of mom and pop stores and the U.S. Postal Service. Newspapers, polite discourse, all going the way of the honeybee. It was the last moment in human history before a new age of the internet and everything that came with it.

DANIEL (CONT'D): Before we learned how to digitize our personalities, our memories, our very souls, and download them into some poor dead person. As much as people today willingly partake in those things, they yearn for a simpler time.

PHILLIP: They did.

DANIEL: They will again. Everything is cyclical. I think it's the right time to get my novels back out there. Let them all know I'm still here. And then I'll be inspired to start writing again.

PHILLIP: Good luck. Hey, you should hurry up and get a new module before all the publicity starts up again. You can't go out there looking like that.

DANIEL: Don't start.

PHILLIP: Seriously, Danny. Don't you miss being young? What are you gonna do? Just die in that thing?

DANIEL: Of course not.

Daniel lifts the wine bottle to him.

PHILLIP: Half a glass. I'm still getting used to being 120 pounds lighter than I was last week. My first night out on the town was a shit show. I literally woke up in a gutter.

DANIEL *(laughs)*: I've been there.

PHILLIP: Damn right, I pulled you out of a couple. Back when you were fun. Sucks, man. What are the odds that your birth body and the guy you moved into would carry the gene for being a drunk?

DANIEL: Getting a new module might work for beating Parkinson's or tennis elbow, but some diseases follow you from body to body.

PHILLIP: Fine, but that's not a good enough excuse for dragging your feet. Seriously man, what are you waiting for?

DANIEL: In case you haven't noticed, these things aren't cheap.

PHILLIP: No shit. I'll be paying this one off until I'm an old lady. Seriously, like, thirty-five. But who cares?

DANIEL: Money's no object, right?

PHILLIP: No! I mean, of course it is for the other half, squirming like swarms of rats in those megacities, drinking rust water and praying that the entire electrical grid doesn't go down for good this time.

DANIEL: The other half? Your math is off by about 49 percent.

PHILLIP: We ain't them, is my point. Why not treat yourself to more than a popsicle?

DANIEL looks at his friend like he might confide in him, then:

DANIEL: Speaking of possible good news, I need to connect and see if my agent called.

PHILLIP pours himself a little more wine as DANIEL opens a virtual window and disengages offline mode, talking as he does.

DANIEL (CONT'D): I can't believe I'm going to ask this, but... what's your plan with this big change? When it comes to... dating?

PHILLIP: Oh! I'm straight, man. Nothing but vagina for me.

DANIEL: Okay, let's see... an email about my airline miles expiring, junk, junk, junk, ten unanswered calls from Al along with three voicemails that I'm going to go ahead and delete...

He stops. PHILLIP notices.

PHILLIP: Did your agent call?

DANIEL: Uh. No. I just need to listen to this voicemail. Excuse me.

Silence as DANIEL is obviously affected by what he's hearing.

PHILLIP unconsciously rubs his body with his hands. DANIEL closes the virtual window and stares.

PHILLIP: Everything all right?

DANIEL: Yes. But I think I need to tend to some things.

PHILLIP: Yeah, sure. What am I doing wasting time here anyway? Look at me. The world is my oyster. As long as I make sure no one slips anything into my drink at the bar. Hey, I know all the tricks, because I've used them! Right, old pal?

DANIEL: I'm thinking this is going to be quite the eye-opening experience for you, Phil.

PHILLIP: Before I go, just look at this, will ya?

PHILLIP lifts his shirt and flashes DANIEL. Daniel catches a glimpse before he realizes what's happening, screams and covers his face. Phillip laughs and heads to the exit on wobbly legs, throws the door open, turns again.

Sayonara, amigo!

And he's gone. DANIEL takes a moment to collect himself. He sits, takes a breath, opens a virtual window, jabs the air a couple times, then waits. After a couple seconds:

DANIEL: Hi. It's me. Looks like we're playing phone tag.

(A beat)

I'm so glad you called. I've been...

(He trails off)

You didn't say much in your message, but you mentioned coming by. I wish you would. Any time you like. I just need to know when so I can have security let you in. It's been so long, I'm sure your clearance has lapsed. I didn't mean for that to sound critical, it's just the truth. I'm babbling. I'm just so...

A beat.

DANIEL (CONT'D): So just let me know when you're coming. I'll be here. We'll be here. I can't wait to... I'm looking forward to it.

(A beat)

I hope you're well, honey. Bye.

He disconnects. Sits quietly for a moment. Leans back in the seat, touches his temple and starts another 1990s indie rock song. He has settled back into the same position as at the top of the scene, staring into the air above him, occasionally swiping the air to the left.

Lights down.

SCENE 2

Lights up on CHADWICK, a tall, handsome 24-year-old African American, engaging in what looks like some kind of martial art. He's terrible at it, punching and kicking at the space in front of him with no grace or skill, shrieking and hollering at the top of his voice.

DANIEL enters from the hallway and sees this, utterly confused.

DANIEL: Excuse me.

CHADWICK continues unabated. DANIEL approaches him.

Excuse me!

Startled, CHADWICK nearly attacks DANIEL, who cowers and falls the ground.

CHADWICK: Oh shit.

CHADWICK touches his temple with a COMPUTER TONE and looks around, sees DANIEL.

Damn, dad. Be careful!

DANIEL: Chadwick?

CHADWICK: You shouldn't go sneaking up on people. I was playing Jymberwocky.

DANIEL: Playing what?

CHADWICK: Do you live on this planet? Jymberwocky. The virtual adventure fighting game. I was battling the Poison Pandas. For a second I thought you were King Tai Shan.

DANIEL looks CHADWICK up and down.

What?

DANIEL: Just taking this in.

CHADWICK: Oh yeah! Dome, huh?

DANIEL: Dome?

CHADWICK: An urban term meaning superlative, magnificent, or—

DANIEL: I get it. Say, did you put any real thought into this?

CHADWICK: How do you mean?

DANIEL: I'm asking if you comprehend the gravity of this choice.

CHADWICK: Who wouldn't want to be black if they had the choice? It was a slam dunk! No pun intended.

DANIEL: Do you know the first thing about the culture that you've just appropriated?

CHADWICK: I know everything I need to know. For instance, there isn't one thing that white people invented that black people didn't do better. Baseball! Jazz!

(Struggling to come up with another example)

...Potato salad!

(Suddenly changing his argument completely)

Besides, I don't see color.

DANIEL: Your mother tells me you fell out of a helicopter.

CHADWICK: Oh, yeah! I screamed like a bitch the whole way down. You wanna see the video? I'll send it to you.

DANIEL: Don't. Did it occur to you to ask me if it was okay to get a new module?

CHADWICK: No. I'm an adult.

DANIEL: It's so easy to forget. You know, Chad, the 30s are great. It's the peak of a man's maturity. You should let yourself get there some time.

CHADWICK: I'll just take your word for it.

DANIEL: Happiest time of my life. I was successful. Your mother and I were still newlyweds. You and Dee were babies. My whole life was ahead of me.

CHADWICK: It still is. Get a new module and do it again. Start at 30 if you want. You can get one of those dirt cheap. You can have this one for almost nothing in a few years after the shit I'm gonna do to it.

AL enters through the front door. She sees CHADWICK and squeals with delight.

AL: There he is!

CHADWICK: Here I am!

She looks him over and then they embrace.

DANIEL: You're late, Alice. She'll be here any minute.

AL: I know! I just need to freshen up. We'll celebrate this later, Chadwick. I watched your video! You screamed like a bitch!

CHADWICK: The whole way down!

She quickly goes to the wet bar and pours herself a huge glass of wine then exits down the hallway.

Who's coming?

DANIEL: Your sister.

CHADWICK *(moaning)*: Yo, for reals?

DANIEL: For reals. Say, I don't imagine you'll be paying for this out of your own pocket.

CHADWICK: Not likely!

CHADWICK opens a virtual window, begins swiping and poking.

DANIEL: Do you have any idea how much these bodies cost?

CHADWICK: Mom's got it covered.

DOORBELL.

DANIEL: She's here.

No reaction from CHADWICK, still swiping.

She's here!

CHADWICK: What am I supposed to do? Stand at attention?

DANIEL: Chadwick!

CHADWICK disengages from the virtual window and sits in a huff. DANIEL centers himself, then opens the door, revealing DEE, a 50-year-old woman. She enters hesitantly.

Hi, Dee.

DEE: Hi, dad.

He regards her, looking at her tenderly, both trying to decide what kind of greeting is appropriate.

DANIEL: It's so nice to see you, honey.

DEE: You too.

She finally gives him a polite hug. She sees CHADWICK on the couch, still occupied.

Please don't tell me that's Chad.

CHADWICK looks at her.

Technology's answer to blackface?

CHADWICK: Yo, sis.

DEE: You're looking well.

CHADWICK: What, this old thing? You look skinny. Congrats!

DANIEL *(to Dee)* What can I get you?

CHADWICK: I'll take a malt liquor.

DEE: Just water, thanks.

DANIEL exits to the kitchen.

Awkward silence.

So. What's new?

CHADWICK: Just pockin' it swole.

DEE: What does that mean, exactly?

CHADWICK: If you have to ask...

(Correcting himself)

Ax...

DEE: Still living here?

CHADWICK: You know it. Why would I ever leave?

DEE: So you can have your own life.

CHADWICK: I have my own life. It's fucking awesome.

DEE: Do you have a job?

CHADWICK: I just said it's fucking awesome, does that not answer your question?

DEE: Bitchin'.

CHADWICK: Man, already on my case. You never change, do you?

DEE: I continually change, actually. I grow older and participate in the process of evolving physically and mentally over time, instead of—

CHADWICK: Here we go.

DEE: —creating a state of unnatural stasis in a completely sheltered environment. But that's just me.

CHADWICK: What are you saying? That I'm lazy? 'Cos that would be racist.

DEE: I'm saying you're an eternal child, completely ignorant and privileged to the point of existing in a fantasy world.

CHADWICK: Okay, well that's fine.

DEE: You know, I'd like to at least believe that you did this

(Pointing at his body)

out of an authentic curiosity about ethnology, and not as yet one more way for the white man to reap the benefits of centuries of struggle without suffering any of the burden.

CHADWICK: Can't it be both?

DEE: Still not serious with anyone, I take it. Just a revolving door of young, dumb-as-bricks blonde girls for a night or two.

CHADWICK: They're not all blonde! Last year I dated a girl from the Philippines. That's right: she's Philippian. And before you ask— No, I didn't order her on the internet.

DEE: It never would have occurred to me to ask that.

CHADWICK: Oh, and I'm the ignorant one?

DANIEL interrupts.

DANIEL: Here's your water.

CHADWICK: Where's my beer?!

Obviously there's no beer.

CHADWICK (CONT'D): Yo, you're both klack!

He turns and starts off, stops and turns back.

An urban term meaning absurd or ridiculous!

CHADWICK exits to the bedrooms in a huff. DANIEL and DEE regard each other in silence.

DANIEL: Your mother will be out momentarily.

DEE: Is she... still...

DANIEL: Oh. Yes. She's still the same as the last time you saw her.

DEE: And so are you.

DANIEL: Yeah.

DEE: I wasn't sure.

Not sure what to say to this, DANIEL just smiles and nods.

I didn't intend to come here and be so mean to Chad. He just—

DANIEL: It's all I can do not to eviscerate him at every moment.

DEE: How are you, dad?

DANIEL: I'm okay.

DEE: Writing?

DANIEL: Sure, sure.

(Beat)

You?

DEE: Sure.

They give each other a little smile, knowing they're both lying.

DANIEL: Still teaching?

DEE: I, uh...had to stop.

DANIEL: Had to...

DEE: There were cuts in the English department at the university.

DANIEL: You had tenure.

DEE: I volunteered.

He decides not to press it.

DANIEL: And how is Jo? I didn't know if she'd be coming with you or...

DEE: We broke up.

DANIEL: I'm sorry to hear that. Is that why you're here?

DEE: No. It happened last year.

DANIEL: That must have been very hard for you.

DEE: It was.

DANIEL: I wish you would come to me with these things.

No response.

Are you doing okay now? You were very vague on the phone.

DEE: I... have had other things to deal with.

DANIEL: Dee, honey, can you—

AL enters with her drink, and for her at least, it's all as if there hasn't been the slightest bit of trouble between the two of them.

AL: Deandra! You're here! Why didn't your father come get me?

DEE: Hi.

AL: Would you like something? A drink? You need to try this cabernet I got from—

DEE: I have water.

AL: Something to eat? It's so close to dinner time, I didn't know if you wanted to stay or have snacks or—

DEE: No, thanks.

AL: You look like you could use a meal, Deand—

DEE: Please just sit. I just want to get this out and then go.

AL: Get what out, dear?

DEE motions for her to sit. AL does, next to DANIEL. Dee takes a moment, then:

DEE: I'm dying. Cancer. Pancreatic, and it's spread, so that's it. I'm not telling you for any other reason than I thought you both should know, and it seemed like the kind of thing I should tell you face-to-face.

She gives AL and DANIEL a moment to take this in.

They say about three months. I've accepted it, and I'm managing the pain—

AL: There must be—

DEE: Stop. There is nothing to be done. Not by you, not by anyone. But especially by you.

AL: Deandra, of course—

DEE: This isn't a discussion. It's me performing the courtesy of informing you. If you want to ask me some questions, fine, but this is not— I repeat, not— an opening or opportunity for you to help, in any way.

AL: Can't we at least discuss options, Deandra? This is ridiculous.

DEE: Options? Let me guess. You want me to go against my most deeply held beliefs and convictions for your selfish needs.

AL: Our selfish needs? We're talking about your life!

DEE: I've already told you I've accepted it. The only reason to try to fight the unavoidable is so you can feel good about—

AL: It's not unavoidable!

DEE: Again, only if you imagine that I would agree to becoming the biggest hypocrite in history.

AL: Death trumps your beliefs. Can't you understand that? You're getting downloaded into a new module, and that's the end of the discussion.

DANIEL: Alice...

DEE: I did what I came here to do. I'm going now.

AL: Fine, go. I guarantee that as the day gets closer, and as what is about to happen really starts to dawn on you, you'll change your mind. And that's when we'll help you.

DEE: I'm not going to change my mind. I'm going to die. I already made the arrangements and I have a doctor and a legal team that have assured me that no one will be able to cram implants in my head and upload me to the Heaven Database. I was hoping this visit could be quick and relatively painless, and I'm sorry you had to turn this into a fight, but now you know. It's not happening. I'm very tired. Good bye.

She is already at the door, when:

AL: It's already happened.

DANIEL: Alice!

DEE: What?

AL: The implants are already in your head, and Life Forever Industries has all your data stored. Even if you succeed in stopping the monthly back-ups now, your data is very current.

DEE: How? When? I...

DANIEL: Alice, don't.

AL: When you had your wisdom teeth out. When you were sixteen. We had them do it then. You were already showing signs of being such a little pain in the neck about it, and we thought—

DEE: I can't believe this. Oh, wait. Yes I can. This is actually very easy to believe.

AL: What if you had an accident? Teenagers are so reckless. We—

DEE: I'm an adult. I can nullify any agreement you made with the LFI people, and erase—

AL: Do you really think you can fight our lawyers, Deandra? And get it all done in three months?

DANIEL: Alice...

DEE: Really, mother? You're going to make me spend the final days of my life fighting a legal battle so I can die the way I want? Are you fucking serious?

AL: I'll do what it takes to keep you alive. That's what parents do. I know in your heart this is what you want. I wouldn't be doing it if I didn't believe that.

DEE: How dare you. You have no idea. You fucking evil bitch.

DANIEL: Dee–

AL: Be as angry at me as you like. I've given you life once, and I plan to keep doing it as many times as I can. If you'd ever had children yourself, you'd–

DEE: I can't believe you let her do this. You have to make her stop. Daddy.

DANIEL can only look away.

AL: Deandra, why don't you make it easy? Help me pick out a module for you. A nice pretty one. Wouldn't Josephine like that?

DEE is about to lash out but she suddenly clutches her back in a shock of pain. DANIEL and ALICE jump to help her but she waves them off, takes a moment for herself, and recovers.

DEE: Do you know why I'm dying of cancer at the age of fifty? Despite eating healthy, never smoking, living as truthful and honest a life as I possibly could? Do you know why for the last 20 years, the life expectancy of the average person has plummeted? Why for the last 40 years, disease of every kind, including ones previously thought eradicated, have flourished? Because people like you don't care anymore. Why would you? Got a bum body with a bad ticker? Get a new one. Oh no, this one has a weird birthmark on its cheek. Next! You think I'm kidding? I know a woman who junked her new module after six months because it had resting bitch face. An upper class that is too self-involved to look after the rest of humanity might as well mean the end of civilization. But why would you care? When you think about it, the faster we die, the better the selection for you! Can't you see what it's leading to? Just look around, because we're already there. This is just one big planet of cattle to sustain the chosen few. I don't want to be around for it, much less have a hand in it. Go ahead and download me into as many new bodies as you want, mother. I'll make sure you see the bloody end of every single one of them.

Done with her mother, she looks at DANIEL, and keeps looking at him until he finally meets her gaze.

She shakes her head in disappointment, then exits.

Silence for a moment.

AL: I hope you know what you need to do.

DANIEL: What?

AL: You were always her hero. Lead by example.

DANIEL: What are you saying?

AL: Show her how wonderful it is to be reborn. Show her that despite your own misgivings, you're able to do the right thing.

DANIEL: She seemed rather steadfast, Alice.

AL: No one wants to die when there's an alternative. You're getting a new module someday anyway, do it now when it might just do some good. It could save our daughter's life.

DANIEL: It will only drive her further away.

AL: So what is your plan?

DANIEL: It's not our plan to make!

DANIEL moves away from her, instinctively toward the bar. He begins to open a bottle of club soda, then throws it against the wall. Silence for a moment, then:

AL: Is what she said the reason why you don't want a new module? Do you believe we're somehow contributing to the downfall of civilization?

DANIEL: No.

AL: Then why are you hesitating, Daniel? Every time I bring it up with you, you shut down. Can you tell me?

No answer. She goes to him, speaks softly.

Do you remember when we first started dating, in the throes of new love, so madly happy? You were living in that shithole of an apartment on Greenmount?

DANIEL: Of course.

AL: Carpeting in the bathroom. What kind of psychotic landlord does that? And the constant smell of pigeon crap in the air.

He doesn't answer, but the memory stirs something in him.

It might as well have been the Spring Hill Suites to me. I would lie there on that springy, creaky bed, just watching you write. For hours, knowing that you forgot I was even in the room, and I didn't care. You were writing the novel that would make the world want to know you the way I already did. I never doubted it.

DANIEL gets a faraway look.

Your hair was getting out of control. Remember?

DANIEL: My hair?

AL: I implored you to cut it, but you kept saying, "Not until the book is done." And you didn't have the kind of head for long hair. Not in that birth body of yours. You were a novelist, not a rockstar.

Daniel chuckles lightly. She turns him to look in her eyes.

Daniel. Was it a better book because you didn't cut your hair?

DANIEL: You think that's what this is?

AL: Don't you remember how glad you were after you went to the barber? "Why did I wait so long?! What was I so afraid—"

DANIEL: It's not a haircut, Alice. It's a major life decision. An expensive one, that shouldn't be entered into—

AL: I know, baby, I know.

DANIEL breaks away from her.

What is it?

Silence. Finally:

DANIEL: It's not me.

AL: What—

DANIEL: It's you. Keeping us alive. Has been. For a while. Used to be me.

AL: Daniel...

CHADWICK enters.

CHADWICK: She gone already?

AL: Go to your room, Chadwick!

CHADWICK exits like a scolded child.

DANIEL: It's not the money. It's what it means. I used to serve a purpose to the world. And that importance was represented by a number. An amount, showing up in our bank account every week. And with that number, I could do things for you, and Chadwick, and Dee. And for myself. Now I'm like a ghost, haunting this place, waiting to somehow become visible again. To mean something.

AL: You do! You got us here! Look at what you've given us. This person standing here in front of you. You gave this to me. Let me try to repay you just a tiny bit of what you've given me. And then, you know what? Then it'll be your turn again. That's the way it happens, baby.

She has come to him, close, holding him by the shoulders and looking into his eyes.

DANIEL: Maybe in a little while, things will switch back. I'll get that call.

AL: Exactly. We'll just take turns, over and over. One takes the lead, then the other. We're a team, baby.

They kiss, then hold each other.

Is that a yes?

DANIEL: Maybe it will convince Dee, somehow.

AL: We can start looking right away. In fact, why don't we try what Phillip did?

DANIEL: What Phillip did?

AL: Going straight to the showroom.

DANIEL: Oh. Right.

AL: Before they even put them up on the site. Scoop up the perfect one before anyone else their hands on it, get it done then and there.

DANIEL: Yeah. Get it over with.

AL: It would be great if you could score like Phillip did, wouldn't it? With that hot little number he found.

A beat.

DANIEL: How do you mean?

AL: I mean... he hit the jackpot. Wouldn't you say?

AL goes to the bar to pour a drink.

DANIEL: Are you suggesting you want me to find a hot little number?

AL: No! I wasn't necessarily suggesting that.

DANIEL: But you weren't necessarily not suggesting it.

AL: I do think you should keep your options open.

DANIEL: Ah.

AL: I mean, is it something you've ever considered?

DANIEL: No, Alice. I can promise you it's something I've never considered.

AL: I'm just saying, keep an open mind.

DANIEL: You want me to download into a female module.

AL: I want you to do what makes you happy, Daniel.

DANIEL: Just a suggestion, huh?

AL: That's all it is.

(A beat)

I think I should be allowed to make suggestions.

(A beat, quietly)

I am paying for it, after all.

DANIEL struggles to remain calm despite quickly rising blood pressure.

DANIEL: And if I say no...

AL: I'm sure you'll realize the best thing to do.

DANIEL: For whom?

AL: For us, Daniel. Things haven't been the same.

DANIEL: Since you became a man? I'm inclined to agree. But we swore that it wouldn't matter.

AL: Well it turns out it sort of does. What can I say?

DANIEL: For a couple that's been together as long as we have, it shouldn't.

AL: What's the point of being forever young if we can't take advantage of it, Daniel? We can have vibrant, gorgeous, fully functional bodies to do all the things that bodies like to do to each other. Don't you remember what that feels like? Don't you miss it?

Unnoticed, CHADWICK enters again.

DANIEL: I'm getting by without it, because it's what you wanted.

AL: Well I can't take it anymore! It's not enough for me anymore, jacking myself off as I suck your dick while you lie there, rigid, with your eyes shut tight!

CHADWICK freezes, pivots, quickly exits.

DANIEL: So let's call this what it is. It's not a suggestion. It's an ultimatum.

AL: All I'm asking is that you do the logical thing. The best thing for this family.

DANIEL: You know, it's astounding how often the logical thing to do is the thing that suits you best.

AL: Well, Daniel. Maybe someday you'll be the one that gets to call the shots again.

Everything stops. DANIEL recovers and heads for the door.

Where are you going?

DANIEL: Out.

He turns to leave, then stops.

You know, I've never told you this before, but out of all the bodies that you've had, do you know which one I liked most? Not that first one, not the second one, certainly not this one. It was the original. I didn't see an older woman, I saw perfection. I loved every inch of that body. The smell of that body. The one that created and gave birth to both of our babies. You can't improve on perfection, Alice.

AL: You did tell me that before. Once when you were drunk.

(A beat)

Go on out. Clear your head. But we need to go to the showroom, and it has to be soon. Remember why we're doing this. For Deandra.

DANIEL *(with venom)*: Right. For Dee.

He exits. Lights down.

ACT 2

SCENE 1

Lights up on a different place. It is the opposite of the Totten abode. This is a cheap apartment that, while kept tidy, can't help but look disheveled and unkempt. DEE stands in the middle of it, looking deep in thought and troubled, arms crossed, uncomfortable in her own home. DANIEL enters from the kitchen holding a glass of water and sees her like this.

DANIEL: Thanks, for the water.

DEE: That isn't from the tap, is it?

DANIEL: No.

DEE: Sorry water is all I can offer. I wasn't expecting visitors.

DANIEL: Really? Looks like you're planning for a party. You've got quite a stock in there.

DEE: I guess I meant I wasn't expecting a visitor that can't drink what I have.

He takes a sip of the water as he looks out the window.

That's all for me, actually. I don't like the drugs they gave me, but I still plan on going out of this life in a permanent haze.

He changes the subject.

DANIEL: This neighborhood sure has changed.

DEE: Yeah.

DANIEL: It's lost a lot of character.

DEE: That's a way of putting it.

DANIEL: I guess this is what they call gentrification?

DEE: Another word might be apartheid.

He looks at her.

DANIEL: Where did they all go?

DEE: I take it you're not keeping up with the news lately.

DANIEL: I couldn't bear it anymore. Can't watch.

DEE: It's nice you have that option.

He moves away from the window.

DANIEL: I think you've got the right idea. I would do the same thing. The end of my life would be one final glorious bender.

DEE: Yeah?

DANIEL: If I'm being honest, except for all the ways that it made me a failure as a father and a husband, I was at my best when I drank. When I was lit, I was the best writer I ever was, I was the most confident I ever was, I was the guy who knew exactly what to say at exactly the right time.

DEE: So it was a trade-off?

DANIEL: Not a fair one, as it turns out.

A beat.

But yeah. If I was facing the end, I would drink up. Maybe try to time it perfectly so I'd be dead just before the downside came. And if that meant the hangover came in the afterlife, well... who cares if hell is a bit more hellish?

DEE decides she's comfortable enough to sit now, but still obviously a bit guarded.

DEE: Well?

DANIEL: Well?

DEE: Might as well do what you came here for.

DANIEL: What did I come here for?

DEE: She wouldn't stop badgering you until you agreed to come here and talk to me, so go ahead and say what you need to say, so I can say no again, and you can go home and tell her you tried. While you're at it, tell her that I called her bluff and talked to LFI. As I presumed, my data is my property and I'm free to do whatever I please with it at any time. Including deleting it.

DANIEL: And did you?

She stops, looks down.

DEE: I mean, it's not exactly as easy as that. There are forms to fill out and things like that.

He just looks at her.

And I will! I just need to have a lawyer look over everything and make sure—

DANIEL: She didn't send me. That's not why I'm here.

DEE: She didn't want you to talk to me?

DANIEL: Oh, she did. But I'm not personally here to convince you of anything.

DEE: Then why are you here?

He thinks about it.

DANIEL: For one thing, I have nowhere else to go. I got a room last night, but...

DEE: You had a quarrel. About me?

DANIEL: About a lot of things. That have been piling up.

DEE: One of the side-effects of immortality.

DANIEL: I once foolishly believed things actually become easier the longer you're with someone. Over half a century, and sometimes I feel like I know her less than I ever did.

DEE: You've stayed together through it all.

DANIEL: Yeah. I don't know, though. This time...

DEE: What could be that bad?

DANIEL: She wants me to become the better half in the couple.

DEE: You can't be serious.

DANIEL: The scary thing is, if I take my pride and knee-jerk reaction out of it, I have to admit it makes good practical sense. But it still makes me ill. Is that wrong?

DEE: No.

DANIEL: I keep hearing I'm not progressive enough. That this is a new world and I'm on the wrong side of history. That the entire idea of any attachment to our physical selves is completely obsolete.

DEE: You can't help how you feel.

DANIEL: Be that as it may, I don't really have much leverage in the situation.

DEE: You're going through with it?!

DANIEL: What choice do I have? I just need to buy some time. Go along with it for now, and then I can get back on my feet. You know how they say if you hang on to your old clothes long enough, they eventually come back in style? Well maybe it works for people, too. My time is coming again. Maybe before I know it, I'm the one that gets to call the shots, you know? And things can go back to the way they were. This is just your mother and I taking turns as we go on through life. It doesn't sound so bad when I think of it that way.

She just looks at him.

Right?

DEE: You came here for something after all. Approval. And you came to the wrong place, daddio.

DANIEL: I suppose you think I should just go ahead and die.

DEE: Yeah. I think you should get old first. And then die. That's the way it's supposed to work.

DANIEL: Who are we to say the way things are supposed to work?

DEE: I don't know. But speaking of work, I have to be at mine in an hour.

DANIEL: You're working?

DEE: I have a job. It's what people who aren't rich do to survive. At least until we die painfully from cancer.

DANIEL: What are you doing?

DEE: It's a law firm.

DANIEL: Christ. Wasn't Starbucks hiring?

DEE: It's fine. Easy office work. Just afternoons. They've been very patient. Some days I'm just not able to make it in, or I have to leave early. I'll work for as long as I can, and then I'll stop.

DANIEL: Dee, please let us at least give you some money. You won't have to work at all.

DEE: I'd rather work. I don't know what else I'd do until then.

She stands.

I have to get ready.

DANIEL: Thanks for the water.

She watches as he puts down the glass and pathetically heads to the door.

DEE: Why don't you stay here?

He turns and looks at her.

For the day. While I'm at work. Get your head together. Maybe we can have dinner together tonight. And then you can head home after.

DANIEL: I would appreciate that. I should let her know I'm okay.

He opens a virtual window in front of him and types a message in the air with his fingers.

DEE: Don't tell her you're with me. You'll just get her hopes up.

DANIEL: Where should I tell her I am?

DEE: Tell her you're with Phil Fain. Having a boy's night out.

She exits to her bedroom. He shakes his head as he types.

DANIEL: Or something like that.

Lights down.

SCENE 2

Lights up at the Totten residence. AL stands center stage staring at the air in front of her.

AL: He's fine. Won't be home until late.

She scrolls down.

That's interesting.

PHILLIP (O.S.): What?

AL: He says he's with you.

PHILLIP's head peeks up from behind the bar.

PHILLIP: Huh. What do you... think he's...

AL: Do I think he's fucking someone else? No. I never had to worry about Daniel in that respect. Now less than ever, with that limp-dicked module of his.

(A beat)

That was mean. Excuse me.

PHILLIP comes to her with a glass of whiskey. He has his own glass of white wine.

PHILLIP: I've already poured our next round, it would be a waste not to drink them.

AL: Please, stay. We can stage our little intervention another time.

PHILLIP: You might not even need me. Danny's a smart guy. He'll probably come home and tell you you were right.

AL holds her drink out and PHILLIP clinks it.

AL: Here's to seeing the light.

They sit, get comfortable.

I hope you're right. Convincing Daniel is one thing. Deandra is something else. Stubbornness obviously comes from his side of the family.

PHILLIP: It's tragic, really. No child should die before a parent's second module.

AL: I'm not asking something outrageous, am I, Phillip?

PHILLIP: Outrageous? You're fighting to keep your daughter alive and for your husband to have a reason to live. Is he... okay ?

AL: I was hoping you could tell me.

PHILLIP: We've grown apart.

AL: He has with all of his old friends. Rarely leaves the house. Constantly complains that all his old favorite places are underwater, and everything that's been built to replace it all is cold and lifeless. He's a real joy to come home to at the end of a long day.

CHADWICK enters from the front door.

CHADWICK: Yo, sorry I'm late. Let's intervene dad!

AL: The intervention's off. We've got company.

CHADWICK sees PHILLIP and instantly transitions to a very white man's idea of how a black man would approach an attractive woman.

CHADWICK: Oh, shit! Yo, what up girl?!

AL: Calm down. It's Phillip Fain.

CHADWICK *(back to very white)*: Oh. Hello, Mr. Fain.

PHILLIP: Chadwick.

CHADWICK: Bitchin' mod.

PHILLIP: Thank you. You too.

CHADWICK: Just got it. I was gonna go Asian. Seems to be the fashion these days. But then a year later it's passé and you're walking around like a schmuck.

PHILLIP: How's this working out for you?

CHADWICK: Awesome! I'm starting to see why they say you never go back. So. If this ain't happening, can I go?

AL: Yes, Chadwick, go see all your little friends.

CHADWICK starts to exit.

Chadwick!

CHADWICK turns to see AL motioning to her cheek. He runs up to her and gives her a kiss. He passes by PHILLIP on his way to the door.

CHADWICK: Oh, hey, Mr. Fain, do me a favor. If I start rubbing up against you in a club, hurry up and shake my hand and I'll back off real quick.

PHILLIP: Believe me, I've already had to fend off a few friends.

CHADWICK *(about to exit)*: Thug life!

AL: Chadwick, please remember—

CHADWICK: I know, be extra careful around the police.

CHADWICK exits.

Now truly alone, a quiet moment as AL takes a long look at PHILLIP, a hint of a smirk on her face. Phillip looks away, shyly.

PHILLIP: So... Danny really can't get it up anymore?

AL: That's not entirely true. Let's just say the intention is definitely there, but the nuts and bolts of it all just isn't completely... solid.

PHILLIP: It's a funny little thing, ain't it? Can't keep it down at the wrong times as a teenager, can't keep it up at the right times as an old guy.

AL: It can be frustrating.

PHILLIP: Not nearly as bad as what I've got going on down there now. I gotta say, I do miss having that little release valve swinging around instead of all this internal plumbing.

AL: I don't blame you. I'll never go back.

PHILLIP: Oh yeah?

AL shakes her head.

Not to get too personal, but do you really get to have the full experience? I'm impressed how you and Dan have made this work, but—

AL: A big reason why I would love for him to do the sensible thing.

PHILLIP: I bet.

AL stares at her drink and decides to elaborate.

AL: We manage. When I made the change, we agreed that after so many years of marriage, sex is such a minor detail, so it shouldn't matter.

PHILLIP: But it does.

AL: It fucking does. My brain may be 90, but this body is in perfect working order and rarin' to go.

PHILLIP: You're a stronger man than I. So to speak.

AL: Not really.

PHILLIP: Oh?

AL: If we agreed sex isn't that important, it should follow that the having of it elsewhere shouldn't matter that much, right?

PHILLIP: So you and Dan have an understanding.

AL: I didn't say that, exactly.

A beat.

PHILLIP: Got it.

AL: You must think I'm—

PHILLIP: Not at all. And it's between us.

AL: I'm not saying it's all the time or anything. Not nearly as often as I could, that's for sure.

PHILLIP: I have no doubt about that.

PHILLIP gets up and refills his glass as he talks. AL never takes her eyes off of him as he moves.

You're doing what you need to do for the good of your family. Don't ever talk to him about it, and don't feel guilty. That's what destroyed my marriages. Feeling some kind of obligation to honesty.

AL: I'm starting to think that's true. You know something? I'm realizing more and more that life only starts to make sense at about 80 years old. No wonder the world is such a mess. Most people die right around the age that everything finally becomes clear. But no more. This is the dawn of a new age where the truly enlightened will continue to live on and spread their wisdom. The question is, will anyone listen?

PHILLIP: Doubt it.

AL: Remember that old saying, Youth is wasted on the young? It's no longer true! Look at us. We've got the wisdom of the ages in these hot young bodies. We are gods, Phillip.

PHILLIP: Praise be to us!

They clink glasses, take a drink. AL never takes her eyes off of PHILLIP over her glass. Phillip giggles and moves away.

The room is spinning a little bit.

AL: Cheap date.

PHILLIP: Just what every man wants to hear, right? Tell you what, I've gotten more tail in the past week than I ever did as a man. And no chance of getting any of them pregnant. Should have done this years ago.

(A beat)

Although...

AL: Yes?

PHILLIP: It feels like something's... missing. Like, how do two women know when they're done? When they're both tired? "Okay, we've had an equal number of multiple orgasms, let's take a break?"

AL: Sounds like a good problem to have.

PHILLIP: Ironically, it feels anticlimactic. It's just a little confusing to me with no cock in the mix somewhere.

AL: Ever think of experimenting?

PHILLIP: What, like a strap-on?

AL: A real one.

PHILLIP: I don't know if I could go through with that.

AL considers this, drains her glass.

Now that you've experienced both...Which do you like better?

AL comes to PHIL as she refills her glass.

AL: I really love being a man. Being dominant. In control. Taking. Overpowering. But, I have to say...

PHILLIP: Yes?

AL: There was something thrilling about being the woman. Being taken. Controlled. Entered.

AL takes a drink. PHIL just watches, his breath a bit shallow. Al smiles devilishly.

AL (CONT'D): Look at you. I have to keep reminding myself I'm talking to my old friend Phillip Fain.

PHILLIP: I must admit, I have to keep reminding myself who I am, Alice.

AL: You should come see my office sometime. Top floor of the Higgins Tower. Corner office that looks out on the entire city, about a third of which my company owns. Every time sea levels rise another inch, the mice go scattering and we buy low and sell high. It's a blast. Fifteen years ago though, it was a different story for me. As a woman in that company all I got were patronizing pats on the head and constant shit-talking behind my back. But as soon as I'm a man, I'm no longer a bitch. I'm "headstrong." A "leader." They had that right. I shot to the top in record time and fired their asses first chance I got. All because of my little... accident.

(A beat)

No one can resist a deathbed request.

PHILLIP: You get what you want, don't you, Alice.

AL gets close to him gives him a hard look in the eyes.

AL: Call me Al.

AL grabs PHILLIP and kisses him hard, passionately. He drops his wine glass. The kiss continues into BLACKOUT.

SCENE 3

Back in Dee's apartment. DANIEL is alone, talking to the air.

DANIEL: Right. Full forward, onward and upward. Okay. Yeah, we'll talk in the morning when I stop by. Thanks again.

He taps his temple to end the call. He thinks, in his own world. DEE enters carrying a glass of whiskey and the bottle it came from.

DEE: Thanks for doing the dishes. I'm exhausted.

DANIEL is still lost in thought.

Dad?

DANIEL: Huh?

DEE: You okay?

DANIEL: Yes. Dinner was delicious. Thank you.

DEE: Do you mind if I drink?

DANIEL: Not at all.

DEE: Good, because I already started.

DANIEL: Your mother stopped after I got on the wagon, but I assured her it wasn't necessary. Other people should get to have their fun.

DEE: Yeah, I'm getting this party started.

...She says dourly as she takes a sad drink.

DANIEL: Long day?

DEE: You don't need me unloading my crap on you.

DANIEL: I'm your father. That's what I'm here for.

DEE: Well, for one thing, I'll never get used to a guy roughly my age saying, "I'm your father."

DANIEL: I don't suppose that's something one ever becomes accustomed to.

DEE: No, not after the shock of coming home from college one Christmas break to find that my father was suddenly 25 again. You'd think the effect of that would have been blunted a bit by my mother becoming a completely different-looking person when I was five years old. But no, turns out it's the gift that keeps giving in the freaking-you-the-fuck-out department.

A beat as this settles on Daniel.

Sorry, this stuff is like truth serum for me. Proceed with caution.

DANIEL: It's about time we talked about all of this.

DEE: Sure, a few months before I die is the perfect time to try to make my life make any sense to me.

DANIEL: You have every right to be bitter about your situation. But you made a choice to handle it the way you did. You could have had it really easy. Look at...

He stops himself.

DEE: Look at Chadwick?

DANIEL: Bad example, perhaps. But there's a happy medium between shutting me out and never moving out. I've seen it work out beautifully.

DEE: Where?

DANIEL: People we know. Other...

DEE: Other what?

He looks down. Quietly:

DANIEL: Other families.

DEE: I wonder what their secret was.

DANIEL: That's the thing. If I went back in time, I don't even know what I'd do differently. Things look good on paper. Forever young, constant renewal. The tricky thing is, when you get this idea in your head about eternal life, you forget that you still only get once chance to be a good parent.

A beat.

DEE: Well, here's your chance to try again.

DANIEL: You'll allow me that?

DEE: I wasn't talking about me.

DANIEL: You can't possibly mean—

DEE: No, Chad's hopeless.

Off her father's oblivious expression.

You really have no idea, do you?

(Nope)

She always has a plan. But you've always been too sweet and madly in love with her to catch on. Think about it. Don't you think mom would just love being a dad?

He gets it, but shakes it off as if he doesn't.

Remember how long she hounded me to have a baby? She actually accused me of turning queer just to deny her a grandchild. Now she gets something even better.

DANIEL: Jesus. That's been her plan all along. She does things in steps. Gets you to see her point on something you never thought you'd even consider, and then plants the next seed in your head, like she just thought of it. She wants to put a baby in me.

He starts laughing. So does she. They laugh together at the ridiculousness of it all.

DEE: Welp. Beats dyin', right?

DANIEL: I don't know. I honestly don't know.

DEE: Yeah.

(A beat)

I don't either.

The frivolity stops and DEE becomes emotional.

DANIEL: Dying is hard, Dee. Don't spend the end of your life pretending that you're fine with it.

DEE: I have to.

DANIEL: Why?

DEE: Because I don't want mom to win. How awful is that? Fucking truth serum.

DANIEL: You're willing to die over this?

DEE: It's not just that. In so many ways, it seems like the right time. Jo is gone. I've given up writing, trying to live up to my father. I'm out of money. My driver's license expires in August.

DANIEL: If you look for signs, you'll find them. Try looking for reasons to live.

DEE: That's the thing. Even without looking for reasons, even when actively trying to block them out, even with all the shit and the feeling of defeat I wake up with every day, there are moments... maybe just one every day... maybe just a flash of sunlight hitting my eyes through the leaves of a tree while I'm walking... when I think, man, I'm gonna miss this.

DANIEL nods.

And I think of the things I could do with my time left, meaningful things. But it all just seems like too much, too late. I don't want to leave anything half-finished behind. I'm terrified I'll fall in love with something. I've bottled up so much of it that it's bound to burst out and spray out over everything if I'm not careful. And the last thing I'll feel is regret that I didn't find it sooner. I don't want that. I might as well be dead already.

DANIEL: What would you do?

DEE: Don't ask me that.

DANIEL: I'm asking.

DEE: I'd get over myself. Get over all my petty bullshit and accept every dollar you and mom are foolish enough to give me. Travel. Write all the things I said I would. Fall in love, a couple more times at least. Even if they don't love me back. Just... fall and fall and fall. I'd get a pet. I always wanted a cat, but Jo was allergic. Yeah. That would be the first thing. A kitty cat. All I'd need is another ten years. Fifteen maybe. I wouldn't want to be young again. I'd still want to be old. I was always looking forward to being old. Is that silly?

DANIEL: No.

DEE: I have to stop drinking.

She takes another big gulp.

Are you going to tell all of this to mom so she can use it to make me give in?

DANIEL: No.

DEE: Are you going to try to talk me into it yourself?

DANIEL: I'm not someone that should be trying to persuade anyone to live longer than they want.

DEE: What's that mean?

DANIEL: I'm starting to realize maybe there's an expiration date on everyone's life that shouldn't be ignored.

DEE: When did you figure that out?

DANIEL: Very recently.

DEE: I have that effect on people I guess.

DANIEL: I just got a call from my agent. I've been waiting on pins and needles for news about a prospect that would refresh me, pick me up, give me new life. Or, it would fall through and make it pretty well apparent that my one shining moment in the sun is all I'll ever have.

Silence.

DEE: And...

DANIEL *(darkly)*: Good news.

Silence.

DEE: Congratulations?

DANIEL: They're republishing all my books. Soliciting literary reviews from all the major outlets about my work and legacy. It's a smaller pressing than I had hoped, and there was no mention of any possibility of my new work being published, but I'll go on a book tour like the old days, and of course the money certainly won't hurt.

DEE is listening, but she has sunk into the couch and her eyelids are heavy.

DEE: That sounds wonderful, daddy.

DANIEL: Just before he hung up, he said one little thing. Just as a footnote. I'm sure he had no idea that it would mean anything to me. He said that the only reason it took so long for a decision is that any really meaningful analysis of my legacy would happen after my death. That's when, after all, the full breadth of an artist's relevance can finally and truly be measured. Until then, no one can really appreciate what I've done until my story's been completely told. Everyone will go on taking me for granted, the way we all do, every day, with every single other person on Earth, until it's too late. And then comes time to celebrate them. That's how things work.

Silence. DANIEL looks over at DEE to see that she has drifted off to sleep. He goes to her, takes the glass from her hand, and covers her with a blanket. As he begins moving toward the kitchen, he regards the glass in his hand, a bit of whiskey still in it. After a moment, he holds the glass up to his nose, takes in the smell of it. Stares at it again. Then, puts the glass to his lips, tips the glass, and drinks the rest, savoring it with eyes closed.

He opens his eyes, resolutely grabs the bottle from the table, and refills the glass. Spying a notepad and pen on the desk, he sits and takes another long drink. He opens a virtual window in front of him and scrolls until he finds a perfect song that he starts, and we hear along with him. He takes another big gulp, picks up the pen and, after a moment of hesitance, begins scrawling on the pad, with difficulty. He looks up and sees a pair of Dee's reading glasses on the coffee table, puts them on, and goes back to writing with much more ease. The lights fade to black.

SCENE 4

Lights up on Dee's apartment. It is morning. DANIEL sits alone, still writing, but somehow much more relaxed. Silence, no music. He is wearing the reading glasses, looking very feminine on his face. A KNOCK on the door causes him some concern; he obviously wasn't expecting a visitor. He quietly moves to the door.

AL (O.S.): Deandra? Are you there?

He moves away startled, but then collects himself and approaches the door, takes a breath, and opens it.

So. This is where you've been hiding.

DANIEL: This isn't a good time.

AL: We need to talk.

DANIEL: I was going to come by tonight.

AL: I don't want to wait until tonight. You walked out four days ago. Except for a few cryptic texts from Deandra telling me not to worry, you haven't answered my calls. Neither has Deandra, but that's nothing new. That fact that I actually came here should tell you how desperate I am.

DANIEL takes a moment, then motions her in. AL enters and takes it all in.

Is she here?

DANIEL: Did you come here for her?

AL: No. Look at this. What she needlessly puts herself through. No wonder she's dying. At least the neighborhood seems safer than it used to be.

DANIEL: What do you want to say?

AL: I understand you needed time away. It turns out I did too. We've been together so long, I think we both got into the habit of forgetting that there's a whole world out there apart from the two of us.

DANIEL's guard drops a bit, sensing a sincerity from her that he wasn't expecting, or isn't used to.

DANIEL: That's true.

AL: I've found myself wondering, what is the point of a life so long if we don't live it entirely? We can do and see and feel things that all but a few people on Earth can only dream about. All but a few people in the history of mankind. What I've learned in this past few days is that it takes real courage to accept happiness. It takes strength. To find that strength, we must open our minds. Forget expectations. Ignore judgement. Break the chains of what people might find acceptable. We're above that. We make the rules.

DANIEL: You're saying it's time for a change?

AL: Yes. Thank you, Daniel. Sometimes it's just so easy to fall in love with you all over again, do you know that?

They share a moment. Then:

DANIEL: I need to tell you something–

AL: I have some things to tell you too. Some confessions. These things will lead to better understanding.

DANIEL: Okay, but I should go first. Listen–

AL: None of it will matter. We're on the same page.

DANIEL: What you have to tell me is water under the bridge, really. But this–

AL: What I have to tell you?

DANIEL: It doesn't matter. Let's–

AL: How can you know what I have to tell you?

DANIEL: Call it intuition. It doesn't matter. You need to know–

AL: A blank page. Do you promise, Daniel?

DANIEL: Sure, who cares? We're moving on.

AL: Moving on.

DANIEL: Onward and upward. So–

AL: Together, forever.

DANIEL: ...What?

AL: Stronger than ever.

DANIEL: Weren't you talking about splitting up?

AL: Heavens, no!

DANIEL: What was all that talk about moving on, new life, all that crap?

AL: We don't become stronger by dividing, Daniel. There's no such thing as addition by subtraction.

DANIEL: Actually, that is a thing.

AL: I thought we were on the same page!

DANIEL: Apparently not. Why don't you tell me your vision of our brave new world? I'm bursting with curiosity.

AL: What's best for this family is for you to do what we discussed. A new module for you. A female. Meanwhile, I'm sure you've done a great job here with Deandra, softening her up. If she still isn't convinced, godammit, we'll knock her out and do the transfer anyway. She'll pretend to resent us for a while, but she'll come around. And we'll be a family again.

DANIEL: Everything you just suggested is exactly what you wanted before. What are the bold changes you were imagining?

AL takes a breath, puts on a salesman smile, and starts in.

AL: To deny the rest of the world of the strength of our devotion seems almost unnaturally cruel. It should be shared. Don't you think? Of course you do. You're a rational person. So is our friend Phillip. Phillip and I have been talking. We helped each other understand this way of thinking. Perhaps at the moment, you find this idea... too revolutionary. I don't blame you, Daniel. But let us help you to see it the way we do. Love is love. We must find and foster passion where we can find it. We must grow our numbers. We must—

DANIEL: Are you suggesting we all engage in some kind of three-way marriage?

AL: You and I would be the only ones actually married. Phillip would be more like... an appendix. We wouldn't call him that. Not to his face.

DANIEL: And Phillip 's fine with this?

AL: Why wouldn't he be? I mean, okay, right now he thinks it'll be just me and him. I haven't had a chance in the last few days to talk to him to fill him in on the new plan, but he really seems up for anything.

DANIEL: What else?

AL: What?

DANIEL: Your master plan. What else?

AL: My master plan is simply for us to have it all, Daniel. As long as we remember that we have our home base: me, you, Chadwick, Deandra— and, you know, Phillip— as long as we always have our family, we can have everything else too. Anyone else. But we always have the foundation. We always come back home. We always have us. And then maybe, through the power of our love, we can grow our family. Do you understand, Daniel?

AL has come close to DANIEL, staring into his eyes, touching his belly.

DANIEL: You delusional monster.

AL: Daniel!

AL pulls away from him, stunned.

PHILLIP enters from the hallway wearing nothing but a long t-shirt that he obviously slept in, his hair a mess. He sees AL.

PHILLIP: Oh, shit.

AL: Phillip?

PHILLIP: Alice! Hey. Um. I'm sorry I've been distant for the past couple days.

AL: What the actual fuck, Phillip?

PHILLIP: Let's just take a breath here, okay? I was starting to think maybe things were getting a little too serious too fast, and—

AL: Are you fucking kidding me?

DANIEL: What's the big deal? You were talking about making this a three-way thing anyway, right?

AL: Not until after you're a girl!

(At Phillip)

This is a real betrayal, you asshole.

PHILLIP: Wait, what?

AL: Until he's in a woman's body, this is the man I married, you little whore!

PHILLIP *(to Daniel)*: She doesn't know?

DANIEL: She's about to.

DANIEL moves toward AL and takes her hand. The TONE. Al moves away in shock.

AL: Deandra, what are you doing inside your father?

PHILLIP: I should... give you two some privacy.

PHILLIP exits.

AL: I don't understand.

DEE: I was coming tonight to tell you in a more appropriate manner.

AL: You and your father worked this out together? To take his body?

DEE: He did it himself. I mean, I had a quick decision to make and I made it, obviously. I'm sorry you had to find out this way.

AL: Sorry? This is fantastic news! You're alive! Now we can get you into a more suitable module, and download your father into another one.

DEE: You can't, mom.

AL: Can't?

DEE: You can't bring him back.

AL: Of course I can. I'm the executor of his estate, which includes his data. And I get to pick the body. I'll have your father back with us in—

DEE: He's gone, mother.

AL looks at Dee.

His account with LFI is closed. He's been deleted from the Heaven Database. He's dead.

AL: What did you do?

DEE: It wasn't me—

AL: Bullshit! Standing there in your father's body trying to tell me this has nothing to do with you? Do you think I'm that stupid, Deandra?

DEE: What are you suggesting? That I made dad kill himself so I could have his body?

AL: You got in his head and drove him to it, you little—

DEE: Why would I do that?

AL: To hurt me! That was what you wanted most. To win. To see me suffer. Well congratulations. You murdered your father!

This stuns DEE. She backs off, tries to recover.

Just ask yourself, if not for you, would he be alive right now? If your answer is no, you're living in a world of denial.

DEE: It was the right thing.

AL: When is it ever the right thing to cut short a life that could literally go on for eternity? Can you please explain to me precisely what is wrong with using all the means at your disposal to make sure the people you love live forever?

DEE: Because it makes you forget that you have to love them while they're here! Life should be fleeting! There should be a constantly-ticking clock during every moment of our lives. We should always be conscious that this all ends, for everyone, and always sooner than we'd like. There should never be enough time... Because otherwise there's too much of it. Don't you understand that, mother?

A moment, and then AL starts for the door.

Walk out of here and hate me forever if you want. But if you'd rather know the truth, stay and find out.

AL stops. DEE takes an envelope from the table and hands it to her mother.

At the very least, you should have this. He wrote you a letter. The night he died.

With some hesitance, AL opens the envelope and begins reading the letter she finds inside. She becomes emotional and sits. A moment of silence when she finishes the letter. DEE comes to her holding a notepad.

You can read this too if you like.

AL: What is it?

DEE: His instructions. The writing becomes messier as it goes. And more eloquent. All legally-binding, as he signed them and sent them electronically to his lawyers and Life Forever Industries. He thought of everything. He had a busy night.

AL: How did it happen?

DEE: He died doing what he loved. Drinking.

(A beat)

If you ever really loved him, or me, you'll never tell anyone. Let them think it was an accident.

AL: Why would he do this?

DEE: It was his time.

AL: His books are being republished.

DEE: You knew?

AL: I called his agent, to see if he knew where he was. He told me the good news.

(A beat)

I was sure he was leaving me.

DEE: So you came to entice him with dreams of a three-way marriage between you and his best friend?

AL: I knew he was unhappy. I wanted to give him possibilities.

DEE: You just figured you'd present him with what you wanted, and work from there if he balked?

AL: I'm a saleswoman, Deandra. There's an art to bargaining.

PHILLIP sheepishly enters, now dressed, gathering a few belongings scattered in the room before making an awkward beeline for the door.

PHILLIP: Excuse me, ladies! Hate to interrupt. But I really must be heading out. So nice to see you both. Alice, so sorry for your loss. We'll talk soon. Dee, thank you so much for the... hospitality, and we'll also talk soon. Ciao, copains.

And he's gone.

AL: How did that come about, exactly?

DEE: Pure luck. We ran into each other. Naturally he came up to me thinking I was dad, I told him the bad news, then we went and had a few drinks to catch each other up on the whole situation— including his little thing with you— and then before I knew it, we were back here making things extra weird in the best way possible. I'm choosing to not even think about the myriad levels of how messed up it was to use my dad's body to fuck the female version of my dad's best friend, and how much we were both getting off on that.

AL: And now you'll do what? Pretend to be him? There are laws against that, you know.

DEE: His death will be announced tomorrow. Couple days after that, the press release about his novels going back into print. I'm going to represent him, go on a book tour, as his daughter. A little weird, considering I'll be in his body, but probably not any weirder than anything else that's going on in the world these days, right? And then maybe I'll try to get a couple of my own books out there. And I'll live twenty, thirty years more years or so. I'll get to see the world. I'll get to do all the things I could have done if I wasn't too busy being bitter and complaining about my raw deal the whole time.

AL is quiet.

I'm sorry. I really didn't want you to find out this way.

AL: It's impossible to believe he's really gone with him standing in front of me.

A beat as she takes it all in.

AL (CONT'D): I've lost it all.

DEE: You still have Chadwick.

AL heaves a sigh.

We're both starting over.

AL: You'll be fine. Every day when you look in the mirror, you'll see your father. That's a good thing. When you wake up one day to see a stranger looking back at you, and then a different stranger again a few years later, and again a few years after that, it's pretty easy to lose yourself. I was a good person once. She was the person your father fell in love with. He kept seeing that good heart no matter what body it was in.

DEE: Now that I'm looking through his eyes, I think I can see it too.

AL manages a small smile.

AL: Twenty or thirty more years, huh?

DEE nods.

Maybe that will be enough time.

AL starts toward the door.

DEE: I was gonna go out today and get myself a kitten.

AL: You don't want to do that. That body is allergic.

DEE: Are you serious?

AL: We had to get rid of Francine after your father was downloaded.

DEE: You told me Franny died! I came home from college, you and dad were suddenly my age, and my cat was dead.

AL: We couldn't bear to tell you we gave her away to a nice family that lives on a farm.

DEE: So basically you told me the exact opposite lie that parents usually tell their kids?

AL: If it helps, she's long dead now.

DEE: Anyway, I was going to invite you to come with me to the animal shelter, but you ruined that, so...

AL: What are you going to do instead?

DEE: Maybe just take a walk.

AL: A "walk"?

DEE: Want to come?

AL: I have so much going on at work, Dee. Another ice sheet just melted.

DEE sadly nods.

What do you do on a walk?

DEE: Seriously?

AL: It's been a while.

DEE: Just look at things.

AL: Sounds boring.

DEE: I suppose. But you never know when you might experience something that makes it all worth it. Seeing how a dog on a leash reacts to hearing an approaching fire truck. The scent in a sudden breeze that reminds you of the house you grew up in. A little boy dressed as a princess and his dad who seems thrilled just to see him happy. Or maybe just the way the sunlight hits your eye when it shines through the leaves of a tree. There's something everywhere you look, if you just keep your eyes open.

A beat.

AL: Well. How can I possibly go to work now?

DEE smiles. AL opens the door and mother and daughter exit to the world.

Lights down.

ABOUT STAGE RIGHTS

Based in Los Angeles and founded in 2000, Stage Rights is one of the foremost independent theatrical publishers in the United States, providing stage performance rights for a wide range of plays and musicals to theater companies, schools, and other producing organizations across the country and internationally. As a licensing agent, Stage Rights is committed to providing each producer the tools they need for financial and artistic success. Stage Rights is dedicated to the future of live theatre, offering special programs that champion new theatrical works.

To view all of our current plays and musicals, visit:

www.stagerights.com

Made in the USA
San Bernardino, CA
02 August 2020